TO

_____

FROM

_____

DATE

_____

GIRLFRIEND CONNECTIONS

Moments of Laughter

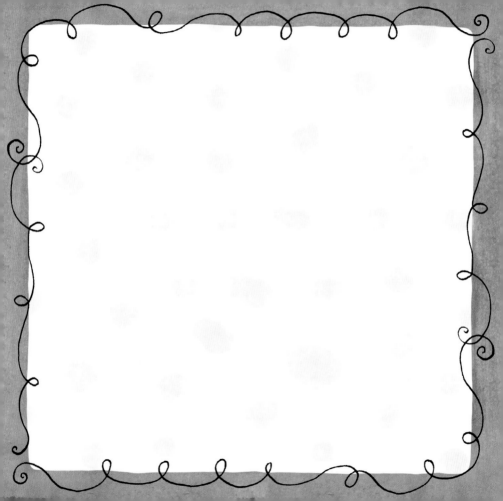

GIRLFRIEND CONNECTIONS

Moments of Laughter

by Bonnie Jensen

BARBOUR
PUBLISHING™

ISBN 1-59310-620-3

All scripture quotations, unless otherwise indicated, are taken from the Holy Bible, New International Version®. NIV®. Copyright © 1973, 1978, 1984 by International Bible Society. Used by permission of Zondervan. All rights reserved.

Scripture quotations marked MSG are from THE MESSAGE. Copyright © by Eugene H. Peterson 1993, 1994, 1995. Used by permission of NavPress Publishing Group.

Scripture quotations marked TLB are taken from The Living Bible copyright © 1971. Used by permission of Tyndale House Publishers, Inc., Wheaton, Illinois 60189. All rights reserved.

Scripture quotations marked KJV are taken from the King James Version of the Bible.

Illustrated by Julie Sawyer. Designed by Greg Jackson.

Published by Barbour Publishing, Inc., P.O. Box 719, Uhrichsville, Ohio 44683
www.barbourbooks.com

*Our mission is to publish and distribute inspirational products
offering exceptional value and biblical encouragement to the masses.*

 Member of the
Evangelical Christian
Publishers Association

Printed in China.
5 4 3 2 1

Laughter. . .

Smiles. Giggles. Out-of-breath, tears-rolling-down-the-face laughter. In the company of girlfriends it doesn't matter how silly we look or whether we're wearing waterproof mascara. We love to laugh together. It allows us to be completely vulnerable for a moment, and in that moment, we share a special closeness. This little book brings to light the significant role laughter plays in our relationships and its ability to form a unique connection between girlfriends. . . . It's a valuable affirmation of God's promise: "A cheerful heart is good medicine" (Proverbs 17:22).

$\mathcal{M}$ake time for laughter

with your girlfriends every day.

Squeeze the joy out of every moment!

A happy heart makes the face cheerful.

PROVERBS 15:13

When grace is joined with
wrinkles, it is adorable.
There is an unspeakable
dawn in happy old age.

VICTOR HUGO

We cannot really love anybody
with whom we never laugh.

AGNES REPPLIER

Girlfriends have a way of bringing

a smile to our face on the bluest of days.

K. WILLIAMS

The happiest days are spent appreciating
the simplest joys with your girlfriends.

$\mathcal{B}$e the spark that ignites

your friends' laughter.

Girlfriends just know. . .
The combination of shopping, chocolate,
and lots of laughter is a guaranteed
cure for almost anything!

Girlfriends always know how to
make even the most dull outings fun.

Every now and then, it's delightful to have the kind of laugh that makes your stomach jiggle. . .that sends tears down your face and causes your eyes to squint so it's impossible to see!

Laughter is the gift of love,

the music of the soul. . . .

KELLY EILEEN HAKE

Mirth is God's medicine.
Everybody ought to bathe in it.

HENRY WARD BEECHER

The art of being happy lies in the power of extracting happiness from common things.

HENRY WARD BEECHER

In elementary school, we loved doing what we
had fun doing. . . . In high school, we wanted
nothing more than to be with our friends—
talking and laughing together. . . .
As we grew, the time between good bouts of fun
and laughter grew, too. . . . But its value remains
immeasurable—as it always will be—because
there are few things in life as important as
joy, friends, and the sound of laughter.

The highlight of a
"most embarrassing moment"
is talking and laughing about
it with our girlfriends.

*G*irlfriends are for leaning on. . .

laughing with. . .and confiding in.

They are one of the sweetest joys of life.

Memories filled with laughter are the ones
we tend to recall over and over again.
They hold the unique ability to be just as much
fun (sometimes even more!) on the "replay."

Laugh with your happy
friends when they're happy;
share tears when they're down.

ROMANS 12:15 MSG

I love you for the part of
me that you bring out.

ELIZABETH BARRETT BROWNING

$\mathcal{B}$ringing joy to a friend is one of life's greatest pleasures.

Girlfriend time is happy time.

Girlfriends understand the
healing properties of laughter, chocolate,
and a good, long shopping trip.

Girlfriends are the ones you
can laugh AND cry with—
sometimes in the same conversation.

A friend loveth at all times.

PROVERBS 17:17 KJV

*F*riendship improves happiness
and abates misery by doubling
our joys and dividing our grief.

JOSEPH ADDISON

*F*riends are as companions on

a journey who ought to aid each other

to persevere in the road to a happier life.

PYTHAGORAS

We should give laughter
a place in each of our days. . .
and girlfriends a special place in our hearts.

It's a given. . .

Girlfriends invented giggling.

Laugh and be well.

M. GREEN

Joining in the laughter and
delighting in the humor of life
with girlfriends easily invigorates
spirits and lightens souls.

Little deeds of kindness,
little words of love,
Help to make earth happy
like the heaven above.

J. FLETCHER-CARNEY

Memories wrapped in laughter

are a joy to reopen.

Unless each day can be looked
back upon by an individual as one
in which she has had some fun, some joy,
some real satisfaction, that day is a loss.

ANONYMOUS

If you can eat today, enjoy the sunlight today,

mix good cheer with friends today,

enjoy it and bless God for it.

HENRY WARD BEECHER

When you rise in the morning,
form a resolution to make the day
a happy one to a fellow friend.

S. SMITH

A good laugh is sunshine in a house.

UNKNOWN

No matter what kind of disaster takes place—
a bad dye job from the salon, a rip in a pair of jeans
while in public, a spilled drink at the lunch table—
girlfriends find ways to turn the seemingly serious
into the most humorous situations ever.

Girlfriends know:

The only thing that outlasts a bad

haircut is the ability to laugh about it.

God equips our girlfriends with the
unique capacity to lighten difficult
circumstances with a little laughter
and lots of encouragement.

That action is best which procures the greatest happiness for the greatest numbers.

FRANCIS HUTCHESON

Unshared joy is an unlighted candle.

SPANISH PROVERB

God has given each of you some special
abilities; be sure to use them to help
each other, passing on to others
God's many kinds of blessings.

1 PETER 4:10 TLB

Laugh, if you are wise.

LATIN PROVERB

It is a comely fashion to be glad—

Joy is the grace we say to God.

JEAN INGELOW

I count myself in nothing else so happy

as in a soul remembering my good friends.

WILLIAM SHAKESPEARE

With girlfriends, laughter
usually outlasts the conversation.

$\mathcal{G}$irlfriends always seem to find

something to laugh about—and they also find

it pretty easy to laugh about nothing at all.

Girlfriends are blessed doubly

when their gab sessions

are interrupted by laughter.

Good friends help us maintain a
healthy sense of humor. When we need
to laugh at ourselves, they make us
feel like it's okay. . .and because
they understand, it's never
offensive when they join in.

Laughter flows in a violent riff
and is effortlessly melodic.

*A*mong those whom I like or admire,

I can find no common denominator,

but among those whom I love, I can:

All of them make me laugh.

W. H. AUDEN

The hearts of friends

are never so quickly joined as

when they laugh together.

Cheerfulness is the offshoot of goodness.

CHRISTIAN NESTELL BOVEE

We occasionally have moments when
we're perfectly content to feel gloomy.
We may even convince ourselves that we
somehow "deserve" to feel that way. . . .
Then along comes a friend who manages to
encourage a smile, and if she tries really hard,
can even send you into a fit of laughter.

ANITA WIEGAND

Laughter is a remedy for every sorrow.

We all need lunch breaks with our girlfriends. It's like inserting a "spirit-lifter" in the middle of our day.

Laughter is the shortest distance between two people.

VICTOR BORGE

Ever notice that when you have one of those

"I can't stop laughing" episodes,

there's usually a girlfriend involved?

With mirth and laughter
let old wrinkles come.

WILLIAM SHAKESPEARE

God gives the blessings of friendship

and laughter; they're both good for the soul.

Silliness is a by-product
of having girlfriends.

Girlfriends just know. . .
Laugh now; laugh later.

We can laugh about our children,

our grandchildren, and

ourselves—we are girlfriends.

Laughter + Girlfriends = Pure Joy

When we reflect on the best times we've shared with our girlfriends, we may forget exactly what it was we laughed so hard about. . .but we'll always remember the laughter.

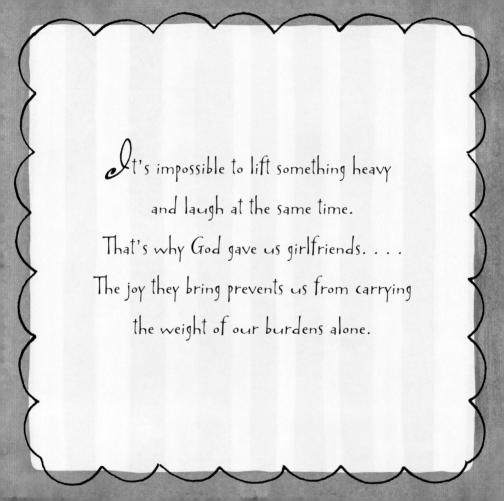

*I*t's impossible to lift something heavy
and laugh at the same time.
That's why God gave us girlfriends. . . .
The joy they bring prevents us from carrying
the weight of our burdens alone.

Worry weighs us down;

a cheerful word picks us up.

PROVERBS 12:25 MSG

Girlfriends and uncontrollable laughter
are one of life's greatest combinations—
like cake and ice cream; peanut butter
and jelly; and popcorn and a movie.

Laughter need not be cut out of anything,

since it improves everything.

JAMES THURBER

God is good all the time. . .and
much of the time His goodness is
poured out into our lives through the
love, acceptance, and laughter of friends.

Girlfriends create laughter—
it's a by-product of hearts that are
deeply connected and joined
together by a gracious God.

$\mathcal{A}$ little time for laughter,

A little time to sing,

A little time to be with friends

will cure most anything.

There are kind hearts still for friends to fill. . . .

ROBERT LOUIS STEVENSON

There's something wonderful about
making our girlfriends laugh.
Maybe it's the sound we love to hear. . .
or the joy we feel in brightening their
world for just a moment.

Girlfriends just know. . .

You can't go shopping for a bathing

suit after lunch without giggling

(in mock-horror) in the

dressing room about the snug fit.

I may have chosen my friends,
but the strength of the bond between
us was beyond my control.

ANITA WIEGAND

When we count the blessings
God has given, we should count
our friends twice—and those who
bring us laughter, twice more.

Learn how to feel joy.

SENECA

The sweetest lives are those
that bring laughter to others.

The best and most beautiful things
in the world cannot be seen or even touched.

They must be felt with the heart.

HELEN KELLER

The path that leads to joy is
filled with friends and laughter.

God's goodness to us is

revealed in our friendships. . . .

They hold the blessings we were created

to enjoy but can't possibly number—laughter,

encouragement, compassion, generosity,

forgiveness, and love.

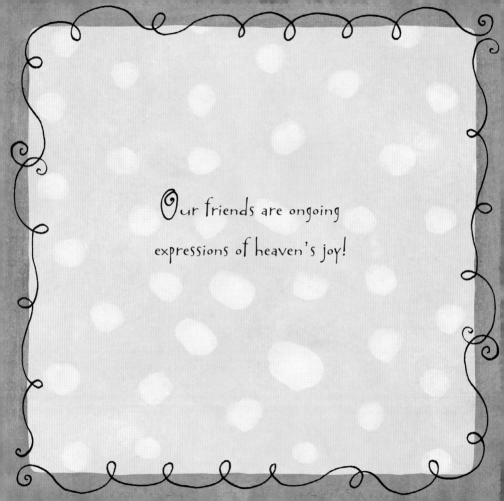

Our friends are ongoing

expressions of heaven's joy!

Laughter is not at all a bad
beginning for a friendship,
and it is far the best ending for one.

OSCAR WILDE